FREE VERSE FOR A FREE MIND

Robert MacIsaac

Free Verse
for a
Free Mind

EVERY BOOK PRESS

OREGON HOUSE

MMXI

ISBN 978-0-9653415-1-6

Book Design by William Bentley.

Contents

for Walter

If I Hold This Pen

If I hold this pen, and if I watch
Each particular syllable expel itself
From every graven thought, or every flitting word,
And mouth, and eye that wants to speak itself;
If I move this pen in rhythms of the heart,
If music moves, and moves to blank paper,
Moves from the burning, and the joy, and moves
To the flying words, and letters, and eyes,
And sounds, and moves to the certain habit
Of stroking blank paper, stroking, marking
What was blank to what forms teeming rhythms
Of what the mind and heart conspire to say;
And my heart is speaking, wants to offer
It to you, and it ripples my fingers
With telling; and we speak, and I hear you,
And I speak; and again I am speaking;

And if I hold this pen, still, very still,
And O so lightly – lightly – just to touch,
Just touch – trembling to tease the weightless dust –
And the rhythms swirling, burning, aching
To move this pen, or move my parted lips;
My heart ripples, and my pen, and my pen,
And if I see this pen, this touch, I see
This – and the swirling, burning wants to speak –
Wants, and wants; and if I always want to,
If I always want – but always trembling,
Trembling, teasing the quiet air, blank air,
And the rhythms trying to write themselves,
Pour themselves upon the blank, and so they pour;

And if they see this pen, this hand, trembling,
And if they saw forever – forever – then, only then, only, and
    to always

See – always – just see; I am seeing this,
And rising where my heart is touching what
I am, and I am seeing love, I want
And I hold you, I hold this, I hold but
I pour away; they see the pen holding,
Press, press paper, O press

What was it, resting in your eyes? You saw
The hills and tapered trees, and crawling buds
Of cattle on the green. And then the clouds
Careened in silence in the sun. You sat,
And looked, and then relaxed and saw your hands
And legs, and tasted sweet air; saw your brow,
The eyes relaxed inside themselves, and watched
Your body feel your burning eyes. They closed.
They ached with warmth. You see your mind unfold
The million tongues. They open. You see them
Open, and there are the clouds, and cattle,
And the million tongues remember cattle,
With their polished horns and lazy mouths;
Again you see the hills and tapered trees,
And see your palms moisten and tapered trees,
And see your tense shoulder and those green hills,
And see your posture and the oozing clouds,
And you blink your eyes. And you blink your eyes,
And you see your cool face, and clouds and hills
Are silent. And you are silent. What was
It then? What was it, resting in your eyes?

○ One Hand Clapping

Lately, I've been wondering about this one hand clapping
    business,
The zen-o-gram that explains it all.
If only we knew what that sage meant – if only we knew.
What separates us from his meaning, his world?
It could simply be, of course, that he's living on the Eastern half
    of the Big Brain.
And we cowboys do all the tongue wagging.

Anyway, I was thinking about this while I walked around town
    today.
I passed many a person on the street,
And now and then our eyes met.
There were frenzied eyes, curious eyes, lonely eyes, blank eyes,
    dreamy eyes, angry eyes, smiling eyes, worried eyes, running
    eyes, looking eyes, greeting eyes, murky eyes, wandering eyes.
No seeing eyes (except a dog).
Each pair of those little windows seemed to have something to say
    – but I wasn't always listening.

Afterward, I was waiting in line at the bakery to order a sandwich;
There were many other legs waiting in line as well.
Some in front of me, some behind.
We waited. And moved. And waited. And moved. And waited.
    And moved. And waited. And moved. And waited. And moved.
    And waited.
We waited and waited. People wait a lot.

So I had lunch in the park and ate my sandwich.
I enjoyed tasting it. And looking around.
Many other mouths had brought their sandwich along as well.
We all sat and ate. And I began to think: probably in the whole
    Northern Hemisphere there must be millions of mouths
    chewing right at this very moment;
Mouths – not many legs. Even fewer eyes. Just mouths.
Chewing the incidental offspring of the Earl.
He probably didn't talk with his mouth full either.

At the end of the day, I got an early train home and at last took
    out my book.
I opened to the marked page, walked to the edge of the
    diving board and plunged in.
While I was swimming around in my ocean of Cervantes,
    I looked out over the many other heads bobbing up and
    down in their oceans of novels and news.
Admittedly I didn't see them too often. I was underwater a lot.
It seems we seldom look at each other while we're splashing
    around.
I guess we're all pretty adept at holding our breath.

Well, after dinner that evening, I went for a walk with a friend.
    It was dark, and the air was warm, and the white moon lit
    the road and trees.
We walked, and talked of little details, things to do, things done.
    I was waiting for the big word. We are friends, and we are
    here walking. I waited.
How would we say it, acknowledge it?
But we continued chatting. You know, chatting.
And yet it was there. Always there.
We are friends.
I didn't say it though.

Raise your hand.
Everything you don't touch, you touch.
Everything you don't hear, you hear.
Everything you don't feel, you feel.
Everything you don't see, you see.

Bravo!

Napoleon's Army at Waterloo

I remember following a god.
I remember his certain manner,
His questioning and decisions.
I remember his glance through a silent crowd,
Seeing and understanding at once,
And doing what was needed.
He would speak to someone, and disappear.
And later we would hear his orders, his wishes.
From mouth to mouth, from soldier to servant,
From wife to cavalryman, from maid to lieutenant,
We all heard and understood his message.
And we marched and conquered together.

There was a path we walked.
We walked with certainty; we fought with certainty.
We broke, we tore up, we raged, we hated, we wept.
But we always won.
Always the struggle, and always the victory.
The bliss of that which resists yielding at last.
The joy of surrender and conquest.
It was so simple then, since he walked ahead.
Our battles followed his, as did our footsteps, and words.
He created a path of certainty.
And along it we walked, and would conquer the world.

Always he was silent. Always we knew him not. We never
    saw him fight, but the fruits were there. He walked
    slowly, patiently, as though on a treadmill, with the world
    moving by him.
And so I would approach, then fly past him, then approach
    again,
And catch another glimpse, and hurtle on.
Always he was there.
We never saw the tempests for the light.
The light shone, and certainty was ours.
Tempests did not exist.

Whenever we fought, we felt his presence.
Whenever we were alone, he was with us.
We were safe.
The furies and their death could not touch me.
I fought, and I was safe.

I was safe.
But today we fought, and we were broken.
He was not there.
No, not before, not during the battle, and not now.
He is gone; and we, alone with them.
They raged so hard, so bitterly.
They were too strong,
And I could do nothing.
But they were always this way, always.
I was always the victor, but I was never alone.
He, my friends, we would conquer. We would!
But we are broken now. And we are here – defeated.
We are walking in silence.
Where has he gone? Why?
As always, no one stops us.
Before we marched where we desired;
The world resisted, and the world yielded.
But the world need not resist humiliation.
But why, why such violent struggle?
What is struggle, when struggle always ends in triumph?
Was this a game? A sport where hounds may rend
Whatever flees or fights, or cowers?
Has all our violent exercise
Only served to burst into exhaustion
And leave us bare and still as tired lovers?
I stare. I am alone. I am alone.

Oh Master! Master! Tell me what to do! You knew, you
    destroyed our fear. Must it return again?

Yet, I am not afraid.
I am defeated. I am still.
I walk through the mist in silence,
And I watch my companions walk.
We are each apart, and silent.
Like the evening stars. A galaxy of defeat.
We walk as he did,
Walking to nowhere, coming from nothing.
Walking, as the world moves past us.
We are here, defeated.
We are here.

There is something which happens to me now and again,
Which I am quite sure happens to you as well.
I mean, it's not so uncommon really.
Doesn't seem to be.
So, I'm sure you'll understand me well enough.
What will you understand? Just this –
I'm walking along the road
(Or, you're walking along the road)
Just walking into town. Maybe carrying a book.
So you're walking (I'm walking)
And you're just, you know, walking;
Swinging your arms, kicking out your legs,
Looking around at the other people.
Walking and looking, and carrying your book.
And so, I'm walking like this, and then I notice...
That I'm walking.
That is, I can see I'm walking.
You know what I mean?
You're walking; and then, you see that you're walking.
Well, that's no big deal.
Certainly you've experienced something like that.
But then, you know what? Something else starts happening.
Something else starts walking.
Right, that's right. Something else starts walking.
Just a little bit ahead of you, in the same way, kicking out
     those legs, swinging those arms, and that book.
Ahead of you, but not really ahead; inside you, but outside.
Something like a telescope, or an accordion maybe.
You just lope along, and then you see you lope along,
And then something else starts loping along –
Right out of your chest.
Doesn't last very long, though, right?
No, I didn't think so.
Does make you wonder sometimes what is really going on.
For instance, if I sit at table and talk to you,
And if I see that I'm talking to you,
Does something else start talking to you?
Right from out of me?
And – well, wait a minute – if you,

If you're listening, and you see that you're listening,
Does something else start listening?
Right from out of you?
And, if we listen to who's listening, and listen to who's
    talking,
Then who's talking? And who's listening?

the rosy maid cools
her burning lids. white waters
surge, like the wild heart.

her mirthful lips press
their quiet laughter – dancing
eyes sparkle kindness.

soft petals nestle
twixt slender fingers that smooth
and tickle perfumes.

she purses her thought,
and kisses her feelings, like
winds warmed by the sun.

her rigid fingers
stroke wispy tresses across
a silent, fixed gaze.

she sways, and pauses
with attentive blush. he sees
his feet push the ground.

they walk through fiery
noon, stand under cool bowers.
shadows hug sunlight.

eyes regard tender
and fall to quick inspection,
adjusting buttons.

I want to say something about honesty.
There are so many wishes that are not honest;
There are so many thoughts, and so many actions, and so
    many feelings, that are not honest;
There are so many things we say to one another, so many
    painful, surprising, shocking things, that are not honest.
I read once in Lermontov where the hero,
After beguiling a young girl with tender words
And quiet manner (but who was he beguiling?),
And not really believing what he was doing
(But is that so?), said to her, "I do not love you."
It is never the truth to admit to a hardened heart, or to an
    indifferent heart.
We do these things, but just because we do them
Does not mean that they are true. They are not true.
Who is sincere can be sincerely wrong;
Who is precise can be precisely incorrect.
It is honest to know this.

There may be something that you have forgotten that you
    would like to remember now;
The hard and fast repose in your breast may not be so hard
    and fast;
There are rumblings, and volcanoes, and rivers of blood
(There are indeed rivers of blood under your breast).
Sometimes it uncoils – the memory of our past –
And in the present hour what had seemed sincere and true
Becomes the insincerity it really is;
Our pedestal and columns rear and fall,
The edifice of an honest, upright tongue.
(Nobody told you, you were lying to yourself.
Maybe they cared anyway, but they did not tell you.)

To be honest is not easy.
Perhaps no one can do it. Yet perhaps it can appear.
Each one of us has an honest hour to encounter.
Many hours. Nothing can sleep forever.
The world uncoils true and burning;

Like uprising columns of smoke, our possessions and
    clothing and principles fascinate, and disappear.
One time a friend of mine was in pain, and he told me,
"I have nothing. Nothing but objects."
That was truly said. But who has nothing?

Glorious, undeniable nakedness. Our friends, our open
    hearts,
And what we must do.

ℰ Halos

Before her eyes it swam and drifted, a perfume of reflecting
   peace;
And as she listened, it was glowing, and it was watching both
   of them.
A face can rest as still as summer, alive without a gesture
   there,
And around it swims the ether, wayward only when aroused.
Around each face it glows or passes, no breath so gently
   drawn as this;
Each face a single mirror, mask, of what lies swimming in
   each breast.
A glimpse, a laugh, a tilting head, and we see this, and
   something more;
An eyelid falls, a trembled sigh, and worlds are spawning in
   the air.
We render, we proclaim the glance, the worlds that sighed in
   briefest space;
We paint the light that mingles us and rushes headlong
   through our blood.

To sing, or fold a paper card, or tuck a rose leaf in a book,
Or stroke your hair, or dip your bread, or gesture broadly at
   the hill,
Or hesitate at other words, or hesitate at words your own,
Or laugh to only pen and paper, or to gaze and wait for tears,
Or assemble cups and pictures, or arrange a table party,
Or rebuke with looking downward, or aspiring, or afraid,
Or preparing tea, or dining (with a napkin touch your
   cheek),
Or the draught of wine that greets you, or the music from a
   page,
Or the draught of friendship taken like a rushing font of fire,
Or alone, alone with others, or with another all alone,
Or watching trees or pensive airs or other things that yield
   fruit,
Or waiting for the word or act that can fulfill what you have
   seen:

These all are ether rivulets curling, curling from the halo's
    arc;
The curling tongue of silent meeting, halo glances, halo
    words.
All men and women wear a halo, all children quiver like the
    candle;
Halos, each a single picture, each a cipher of the breast;
Halos change and halos answer, feel your halo glow replies.
Men and women wear a halo, each corona tells a story.

When we pass, or when we mingle, let it glow ahead of you;
Let it reach, or let it linger; let it choose to be demure;
Let it watch the swallows caper; let it watch the pansies nod;
Let it feel unhappy buildings; let it rise with rising music;
Let it offer up a secret, let it hear one with a smile;
Let it see you, and see others, and let others see it too;
Let it answer when it wants to, let it choose to answer not;
Let it wander through a village, let it wander through your
    heart;
Let it choose, like winter grass, to be as silent with resolve;
Let it gather to itself, let it search for missing strands;
Let it lay you on a mattress, let it push you to a chasm;
Let it show you where to follow, let it let you follow it;
Let it know what are your wishes, let it wish them
    unrestrained;
Let it find, let it succeed, let it love, let it love you,
Let it go – oh, ever gently! – let it go before your eyes;
It will not leave, it dances ever,
Like the flame about the wick.
The flame departs not when it dances, but only when it is not
    fed.

See the halos, they are laughing, even as we start to weep.
See the faces, they are lonely, they are staring at the world.
We stare and see the open world, it never tries to hide itself.
We see parks and sky and clouds, we see bridges, rivers,
    hills;

We see windows, bushes, chimneys; we see bread and cups
　　of milk;
We see mirrors and a hallway; dishes, chandeliers and
　　chairs;
We see statues, carpets, candles; balustrades and mended
　　lace;
Pictures, scissors, books of poetry; vases full of drooping iris;
And clever tongues, and specks of anger; choices, and the
　　wish to speak;
We see an answer, or its meaning; we see the heaviness of
　　death;
We see the tears begin to surge, we see the laughter start to
　　rise;
A glance, a touch, a taste, a look, a stop, a reach, a breath,
　　a wish;
We see it all revealed here, no thing is hiding or reluctant.
We see and stir with other voices, or we are pensive, or
　　ecstatic,
And what we see the halo answers, and what we feel the halo
　　is.
And as the people stare before them, clouds of ether gather
　　there.
What is the rain you are embracing? What is the sun that
　　pierces you?

Every friend and every lover, every stranger or acquaintance,
Everyone who passes by you and smiles hello, or does not
　　this,
Everyone we see before us, on the stairs or from a window,
In the aisles, on the footpath, on the avenue or bridge,
Over coffee, by your shoulder, across the room, or at your
　　breast,
In the park or in the forest, in the city or the tavern,
At your doorstep, through a rosebush, from a tower,
　　or a letter;
Everyone who asks a question, everyone who kisses you,

Everyone who brushes past you, everyone who takes your
    hand,
Everyone who gives you money, everyone who gives you
    service,
Everyone that you have wronged, everyone that you have
    mentioned,
Everyone that you have talked to, everyone that you have
    noticed,
Everyone that you have cared for, everyone that cared for
    you,
Everyone you ever knew of, everyone you ever heard of,
Everyone you have imagined, everyone who spoke your
    name,
Everyone whom you have lived with, everyone whom you
    avoided,
Everyone you have forgotten, everyone you still embrace,
Everyone who understood you, everyone who was not able,
Everyone who told you something, everyone who gave you
    meaning,
Everyone – it was the halo, dancing there before your eyes.
See the halos, they are laughing, see them gesture at the
    world.
Every person wears a halo, each corona tells a story;
Let it go – ah, ever gently! – let it go before your eyes.
It will not leave, it dances ever, like the flame about the wick.
The flame departs not when it dances; so let it dance, and
    dance with it.

A Thursday Morning

She opened the door and said hello.
Her eyes smiled with her lips.
She let me pass and closed the door again,
Then went back to her studies in the next room.
I hung up my coat and went downstairs.
He was eating breakfast.
I made some coffee.
Someone else came into the room.
I took a sip from my cup, then turned and said hello to her.
I joined him at the table.
She cut an apple into pieces and placed them on a plate,
And sat down with us.
We talked, the three of us, about trains, money, theatre, food.
We sipped or ate while we listened, then spoke, then listened
     again.
We talked of ideas, described a feeling, asked a question.
Each of us understood something.
We did not speak when our eyes met.
He finished his breakfast and washed his bowl.
She stared at her empty plate, and I warmed my palms with
     the cup.
I heard footsteps and conversation upstairs.
I thought about my plans for the day.
He walked upstairs, she washed her plate.

And soon I would wash my cup. And tomorrow I would
     remember some of this.
The words we spoke, the taste of the coffee, her pretty hands.
Some of the thoughts we expressed would remain, perhaps
     grow.
The commerce of souls; moving from room to room, from
     day to day.
I see him now, I see her an hour later, I tell her something
     new.
Who are we?
Who remembers? And what do we remember?

Let life be a passion of simplicity;
Let us quietly burn, and float among each other's world;
Let us consummate in quiet around a table;
And let my warm hands touch you when you are here,
And remember you when you are gone.

On Hearing Bach's D Minor Partita

Sliding from morning to warm afternoon,
Friends in bright clothes, and casually smiling;
We visit a gallery and linger in silence,
And then we regroup upon the cool steps.
Only wisps of a cloud, only glimmer and birds,
And slow crowds of people enjoying the heat.
The girls gather sunlight, with fingers relaxed
And hair gently tossed by the whispers of wind.
We pass so much green as we drive through the park;
Luxurious air, and freedom to speak,
Its limpid detachment pervades everyone;
We talk of tomorrow, and watch for a café,
Oh –
Oh, as light that trembles on a wakening pond,
Reflections as busy as the quivering waters,
So now is this moment of darkness and silk;
The smoothness of friendship, impressions of beauty,
But then the dark clamor uprearing itself;
Deep arguments below the rippling surface,
Deep infinite worlds beyond the humid haze,
Forever unknown, forever more real and more demanding,
Forever you sing, forever our picture trembles.

⟳ The Hole Story

I have a hole in my head.
I'm not quite sure how it happened.
There seemed to be a certain buzzing noise inside,
Like some old man talking and talking without end;
And once I heard this buzzing, I just couldn't stop it.

I would sing songs,
Laugh, cry, shout, run, jump;
I'd speak louder than anyone else,
Always interrupt, always ask questions and then answer them
    myself.
Still that voice wouldn't stop!
Next I tried shaking my head vigorously from side to side
And shook and shook until I became frightfully dizzy.
And yet, as the ground reeled and swayed
And I watched the swimming clouds overhead,
That voice just kept on going.
Well, I really became desperate.
I even went and plunged my head into the lake
And held it there 'til I thought my lungs would burst.
But even then, even in that cold, wet, silent darkness
There came that incessant talk talk talk

Yes, things truly looked hopeless, absolutely hopeless.
From morning until night: from the first moment
I peeped my eyes out from under the covers
And wiped away the sleepy crust
To the last, weary, leaden second that I sunk back
Into oblivion – the little man talked and talked and talked.

Until that day when everything changed.

As I said, I'm not quite sure how it happened.
I was slowly walking up the street.
Cars rushed past, children shouted,
People jostled one another on the pavement,
Vendors pointed to their wares,

And I kept walking, slowly, looking and listening
And hearing the little man inside talking and talking.
By this time I'd become rather used to his monotone.
I daresay, I still found the whole matter terribly annoying;
But since all my exertions had come to naught,
I decided I would simply ignore him. That's right,
Let him chatter away to his heart's content,
While I gave absolutely no notice whatsoever.
So, there I was, watching the faces walk past,
Hearing the roar of the traffic, smelling the aroma from a nearby
    bakery...
And listening to the little man.
Yes, listening. For once, I decided, I'll try to hear
What on earth he's talking about (but slyly, of course).
So I kept on smelling the fresh-baked bread,
Listened intently to two little girls singing happily at a window
And verrrry nonchalantly lent an inside ear to the little man's talk.

There I was. I felt, I knew them all:
The sweet warm scent, the happy girls, the incessant chatter;
They were all there, and I was there,
And I listened even more acutely to the little man
Talk talk chatter chatter talk – what was he saying?
What? What?
I looked at the two girls.
One of them, surprised to see my gaze,
Turned quickly away from the window
But came back the next moment and smiled.
The other one looked at me steadily, with a silent curiosity.
The wonderful scent of fresh bread diminished
And – What?! The little man was gone!
Gone?

I listened ever so intently.
I strained with such acute attentiveness
That you would have thought I could hear a flea's heartbeat.
But it was gone, absolutely gone.

At first I let out a sigh and relaxed every muscle,
Waved to the two girls (who merely giggled and went away)
And continued walking up the street.
I couldn't help trying to hear the little man again,
But all that came to me was silence.
I still saw the crowds, the people, all in great detail.
I heard every sound, saw every bird, every gesture,
Every chimneypiece, painted doorway, cobblestone;
I saw and heard and felt and touched,
And still this great silence.

Silence.

Now the silence won't go away.
Now I have a big hole.
Nothing goes into the hole, or comes out.
I just have this big silent hole.
I awake in the morning now and wash, dress,
Make my bed, listen to music,
And the hole is there, big and quiet.
There is noise, movement, talk, feelings
And everything is still quiet.
Quiet.
But, I ask, does everyone have a hole in their head?
I talk to my friends, I make jokes, I say clever things
Just to try and get a reaction, a clue.
But I can't tell.
And yes, everything is so quiet.
And everything is still the same.
I'm not quite sure what to do about this hole.
I can't stop it – there's nothing to stop.
I can't fill it – what would I fill it with?
So I just go through my day, my life
And let the hole go on being a hole.
Holes are very good at that, I suppose.
Do you know?

Of an evening we would wander, bathed in moistened
    fragrances,
Shaggy boughs, curtained with their moss, shading other
    shadows,
Shoots and tendrils, spiky fans, and vines gnarled by careful
    neglect
Brushing as we pass a whisper on arm or cheek,
Wayward roots intruding on our step, the cobbles and curbs
    popped awry about them;
We merge through broad alleés of darkness revealing, breath
    upon leisured breath,
Lusher, deeper groves, quiet in their humid lingering,
Embracing and releasing our meander, unveiling further
    delicious mysteries as we speak and walk;
The set-back houses mute as hammered stone,
Casements dimmed, swings and porches unpeopled,
Only shrubbery and flowers smile back at our gaze:
Roses full or budded or blown, with just seen tints of color;
Camellias winking white amid their leafy folds, like you,
    sudden in their pure appeal;
Unseen honeysuckle exuding sweet infusions, its pungent
    shroud, like you, dispelling what is not this hour –

How say you now?
You sing as though 'twere noon, and sunlight warms your
    creamy down;
You never know darkness, do you? Your day is always,
These whimsical chirrups sage in their unconcern for duty,
Obliged only to unfold your charméd talk in merry lilting
    phrases
Bright with secret, self-involved murmurs,
Free to tell with every throbbing whistle what only silence
    knows;
So close, your cadence lifts and reminds my heart whereon
    you perch,

Your every lucid tone another reason not to wish for what is not
    this next one breath,
You, earnest morning of our midnight, a star somewhere amid
    these crowded eves,
Or slanting boughs, or ivy mantles clung to crumbling mortar,
Or in a hedge, atop the trellis, just there along the stony beds –

Where are you?
I look and do not see, and now I do not hear.
Wait.
There is no meaning in these shadows;
A sky too black stares down on motionless things that lose all
    contour,
And yield neither answer nor question, and cannot explain
    themselves.
This is not the nothingness we seek.

Here you are. I will not move, or look.
Your diaphanous tremors flirt about my sense like sunbeams in a
    well,
The edges of your song a dawn or gloaming that rises or settles
    on my inward gaze,
And now, the hush of each ripened chord heralds a daybreak, and
    day is day.

No matter the years, the places gone, since that time which, like
    all times, was freighted with more than I could know.
That merry light I heard, sometimes just in passing, is at my
    shoulder still, is at my shoulder now –
You who sang are no doubt gone; you who heard are now warbler,
    and heart, and dawn, and morning still.

Someday we may not touch;
Someday we may not need a gesture;
We may not need a smile, or hand on shoulder,
Or turn and indication of the next event;
Someday to meet will be the event itself.
Someday the approach of your modest pace,
Or the recognition of you in a crowd,
Or the renewal on new terms of old turnings,
Or the unrestrained commingling that comes in full ardor,
Someday, and it is almost here,
Is a day when my first uplifted heartbeat,
My first eye-flash of sundry wishes,
That which precedes – and truly is – my smile,
My happy first flush of your presence, a friend, in
    my presence,
Someday this, to you, and the like to me, from you,
Will, in service and in need,
And in everything that has ever made it be,
Touch, and exist, and I know there will be tears.

૯ Midas

He sits at dinner with his face buried in the plate, his two fists resting limply in his lap. There is no sound in the hall, no laughing guests, no idle words and song, no happy tinkle, clatter, no servants hastening with foaming urns to please his cup. No commands. Only the sound of gnawing and labored breathing, and the plate stirring under his lip. Only one servant, mute, frightened. His crown tilts askew, then tumbles on the burnished board (burnished with his curse). He tears and chews the last meat, lifts his head and wipes his lips against the purple robe.

"Wine," he groans and seizes the crystal bowl. The servant comes, but his king holds cold metal.

"No!" he shrieks and hurls it away. It clacks and clatters on the marble floor and rolls to silence. He rises violently and would shove his wooden chair – but it now resists like iron. He flings off his velvet raiment, which clangs to the carpet a golden shield, then snatches the wine jug with his forearms and pours the sweet liquor fiercely into his parched and eager mouth. Now the servant quietly slips away to escape those dire, reckless hands. He drains the vessel and lets it likewise bang to the ground. And again the thick columns and muted drapery receive the brash clamor without echo. Just as the world received his sated wish, silent, unconvinced.

How inauspicious, our satisfactions! And how unconcerned, Life's own momentum! Let me feed on light! Let me ride the wind and tease the coy stars! Give me all!! But you gave me something worse. You gave me what I wanted.

He walks through grey shadows, cold stone, lonely. He ascends the wide and quiet staircase, then hears the merry titter of the maids below, whispering secrets. He watches them, until they see him and move on without looking up. They fear him. They fear a man who has what he wants. He could not know this. He wanted, he craved the thing he suffered to win. Precious coins, gold for food and warmth, gold for wine, clothes, women. The wind scatters dead leaves, and gold scatters men's indifference. Seven coins will buy a kiss, and seven coins are easily won. But whence comes my coin?

He sees tapestries hung dark and still along the wall. One touch, and a bright plate will buy twelve ships. Another touch, another touch, this hard gallery will shine with his fancies. But if his armada comes, what then? If his touch beckons every barrel of grain, every cask of wine, every slave – what then? The world may come silent at his bidding and stand submissive his possession. Could he possess it? Is he more than this?

Hold it. Hold it all, and it will ask your will. You can do whatever you please. Can you? –

He flees the stone and the echo he creates as he dashes into cold air. The stars watch; the sea whispers. No people. The turrets sleep. Only the moon listens.

"I have, and still I want. I do not want this. I do not want what I want. Were I to drag my hands through coarse dust, or race to the shore and plunge the seething ocean into silent peaks; were I to polish this rude earth until it hung a cold star in an empty twilight – where could I go? The golden world would mirror my disdain for what I am and what I have. And still I would have nothing. And still I would want. Dear Gods! Forgive a shadow!"

So he falls, and would clasp his hands, or press them to his face... Yes, he could do this. Perish kneeling, the tomb of his desire. Do we all die this way? Do we not see the golden world we create? A world that gives us what we want, and mirrors our passion or regret? I touch you, and you are mine. Please me. Love me. I will pay with this fingertip. But how we pay, if our touch remains hard! You do not see it all melt and vanish into air. Gold stays pretty, even as we disappear.

He rises, and slowly turns back to his home. He brushes his cloak. It is soft and smooth. He touches the door, and it is coarse wood. And the walls are stone. And he runs into his chamber, and he kisses her. She is warm, and she sees him.

The Statue

He sits so still
He is looking, somewhere
The eyes wide open, the mouth a hint of a smile
The folds of blouse and trousers all carefully placed
Silent light and shadow
He sits full up in the chair
Both arms on their rests
The left hand holds a wine glass
The wrist and hand smooth and delicate
Veins softly bulging under the skin
Fingers deftly encircling the stem of the glass
The vessel polished thin and smooth
Full of pale yellow wine
He raises it to his lips and tastes
How sweet this taste!

4 A.M.

Dark I awoke in the silent dark.
Softly enclosed in my warm blanket.
My eyes were open, and it was dark.
I was breathing. My legs and arms were tired. Motionless.
But my heart was awake.
Someone called me.
Someone wanted me.
I lay silent, still; and my heart was awake.
Reluctantly I moved and rose.
Stepped and waded through the dark
And downstairs to the neighboring floor.
The armchair slept. The hallway gave no answer.
The lamp was not a lamp.
I returned to my bed;
And lay still, and breathed, and grew weary.
And saw nothing.
But my heart was awake, alive.
Bittersweet, yearning, knowing, a slight fear.
(Who are you?
What do you want?
Will we ever meet, again?)

"What do you do when you hate yourself?"
This question was put to me this morning
By a wayward urchin with sand in his eyes.
I asked him kindly to wash his face.
He did so, and asked me again.
I noticed that his shirt was torn.
I asked him to repair it.
He did so, and asked me again.
His tone was somber and unconcerned.
I asked him to speak up and smile.
He did so, and asked me again.
His labored breathing revealed fatigue and hunger.
I asked him to rest and then dine well.
He did so, and asked me again.
He was alone and had no friend.
I asked him to touch someone and look at them.
He did so, and asked me again.
He shook with fear, repressed and smoking.
I asked him to weep and to embrace a stranger.
He did so, and asked me again.
Then there was nothing more. He waited.
"Show me who you hate," I said.

Be not so hasty to untie your shoe,
Be not so quick to tell me what you know,
Be not so – do not rise – where shall you go?
When did it happen? When did we pretend
To pass insouciant through another room?
When was that time, when everything became
One's fingernails: pleasant, unimportant,
And easy, O so easy? The excuse
Was always found in the next endeavor.
A little more, and then we sleep. That's all.
And yet, to rise again was far too certain.
Silence is not luxury for the dead;
It is place. And that place is here. And so
We are quick, and tie our shoes in earnest.
But now you stop. And I can look at you;
And even when you know me like yourself,
And even when we cannot find defense,
Even this is only what it always is.
I am not here, sometimes. I would be slow,
So very, very slow that I never
Could explain what I would do, but only
Do it. Stay with me. I will do the same.

ᴄꞁ Sailing

Allow me to take the helm for a while
The helm of your two parted eyes, I mean
Well it is like a helm really
We throw off the covers and pull away from the dock each
  morning
We cruise through daybreak, lunch hour, afternoon and
  evening
We're always moving forward
The world pulls itself through our eyes and out the back
  again
Or out the top
Or out the bottom, even.
So we are cruising, or plowing, or floating each day
And we are at the helm navigating.
But, are we good at it?
We can justifiably resent someone taking over the helm – our
  helm!
But still, many of us are not good at it.
We don't know where we are going
Many of us don't care
Many more of us are quite certain that we know where we
  are going
(But I don't believe you. You might not even have pulled away
  from the dock!)
So let me take over for a while.
Don't worry, you can have it back soon enough.
Maybe.

So here we go.
For some reason you are reading this
You were floating, or cruising along, and you (sorry, we – I'm
  still here), we are cruising through this.
Where did you just come from?
Well?
Turn around and look.
You can still see the wake you just cleaved.
It's beginning to spread and fade pretty quickly,

But I think if you look hard enough you can still see it.
For my part, before I wrote this I splashed through breakfast,
I came upon a wave of friends, and we sat at the table and
    talked and talked.
With the water lapping at the sides.
I eventually set out into the open sea;
Another friend was going in the same direction
(Coincidence, how I misunderstand you).
And so we cruised in tandem and talked about the weather
And the horizon.
We both went adrift for a while
A long while
Clouds mist missed
Then we came round again and cruised into a narrow river
He went down one fork (to the dentist)
And I am here writing this.

Now back to you (sorry – us).
Have you already decided where you are going next?
How about changing course, just for the fun of it...
What! You grab my arm! You mean, we can't change course?
Oh, I see, you have to go in that direction. So that's it.
But why?
Why is that necessary?
Did you decide to go there, or did someone else?
Here, let me see that map.

How strange.
What a strange map.
One straight line.
Who gave you this?
Well, you can keep it, I don't need that.
But let me ask you something else.
While you're cruising along like this, do you look around?
There are a lot of strange fish around here. And birds.
And clouds, and colors.
Look, over there on the left! See it?

Strange, aren't they?
Yes, I know, somebody already told us what they are.
But that is strange too.
In fact, I don't really care for that.
I've got my own boat to command, and I would much prefer
     to give everything a name of my own choosing.
That's fair enough, don't you think?

Well, are you having a good time?
I am.
Remember, even while you're sitting here as a passenger only,
     keep glancing back at the wake once in a while.
Just to see what we're leaving behind.
Ahhh, this is fun. This is really living.
You know, I wonder sometimes who is really moving.
Us, or everything else.
We certainly seem to cruise from place to place.
We can see things moving past us.
We spy an island in the distance and sail over to it.
We drop anchor and converse with the inhabitants.
Yes, we are certainly moving all right.
I think.
But it is possible, actually, that we are not going anywhere.
That instead it is all coming to us.
For example, that friend you made recently ("recently" by
     whatever timescale you like), the new one.
You found them somewhere, did you?
You sure?
The house you are living in now.
You found it, right?
Oh yeah?
The happiness you experienced some time back.
You came upon that too, didn't you?
Well?
Supposing it had come upon you instead.
And then up and left.
You could try chasing it, or send out a search party.

Shall we cruise around a bit and look for it?
Here, give me the telescope. Let's have a look.

Well, sorry, I don't see anything like it on the horizon.
But maybe it will come by itself.
Like it did last time.

So you see, I'm not actually a very good helmsman.
I should have told you that before.
I believe in the waiting approach.
Yes, because it seems to me that we are not really cruising
    anywhere.
We've been faked out.
Everything else is cruising past us.
It is actually very easy to prove this.
Just try to stop it.
Try to stop what is coming from coming.
Or try this.
Tell me where you are going next.
I mean, right now.
Right now.
And then, when you "get there" and come back, tell me what
    it was like and what you did.
And then look me straight in the eye and say it was just the
    way you planned it.
I dare you.

OK, time for you to take over again.
There you go.
Bon chance.
Don't worry about me, I think I'll just dive off the side and
    have a swim.
Bye!

Intoxication leaves me.
I find myself in search of clothing for a naked fancy,
Styled with capering phrases, succinct as they are lucid;
I scan the air for pictures, like of ladies holding diamonds,
Or sultry avenues in Cairo lined with palms and orange trees;
Of paneled walls in some labyrinthian mansion in Kent,
Of balustrades with flower pots on them, and peeping eyes
     between the rails;
Of wings that ruffle clouds apart
And shed their angry vapors dripping into sand,
Of gnomes and nymphs, and elves on spidery guywires,
Of butterflies, and every measly trifle that can fix the eye.
It leaves me. The mind paints nothing without heart.
An uplifted kernel sits an instant on my pen;
I wait, or I attempt, and either way it goes.

Then there something yet remains.
There is this pen, and my fingers around it.
There is the other hand against my cheek;
My legs crossed under the desk,
Books and statues, and this tablet, upon the desk.
There is my meal, as yet unprepared, and the laundry,
A friend to call, projects to pursue, and among all of this,
Whatever happens next. A dog barks. How quiet the night.
Need I drink my phantoms? Habited in air,
And in responsibilities of time and place,
I am the naked dream I wish to dream.

Pause

After many hours in the heat, it seemed as though I had lost
    myself,
So I sat and rested on a shaded bench, and leaned back
    against the welcome stone.
While I was sitting there, I took delight in watching a cloud
    of hummingbirds about a little fig tree;
In easy pendant play they floated among the coiling limbs,
Looking as though the fruit had unplucked itself, and nimbly
    avoided the harvest.
Down from one branch there hung a plastic feeder,
Where turn by turn before the bright red nozzle
Each eager fellow bobbed in magic place
And took to suck in his silent, desperate manner.
As each retreated, he kept a sidelong dance
From bud to bud, then careened a dizzy circle
Back toward that huge red kiss.
There seemed no wish among them for sky or distant
    perches
Or any migration beyond their crowded circle;
And nothing to calm their purpose and desire.
And then – one stopped.

I saw him hover and drop upon a trembling twig.
His wings receded, and he did not move.
The storm of his feeding friends continued around him,
But he remained unchanged.
I watched – and watched – him. He did not move.
I waited. Another moment and he would be lost amid the
    whir.
Another instant, and he would quiver and lift.
Another second – another second – and he would disappear.
But he did not move. He did not move.
My eyes grew misty and unfixed from gazing.
Surely he would rise away – surely he would return to what
    he was.
Surely he would cease to rest. These creatures do not rest.
And I leaned and watched him, and he still was there.

⟨ Haiku Impressions

the cats danced: milky
white puffballs lolling. soon I
sleep, and dream of you.

little boys run through
sleeping pigeon drove – sudden
wings applaud the sun.

leaves scratch and rustle
on windy asphalt road. Spring
is sweeping up Death.

flurry of black snow
swirls to rest on green hill; up
again, chirping flakes!

sunlight wiggles in
the fisher's net. lattice clouds
cover sea-blue sky.

white swans like questions
watch themselves silently. on
banks narcissus nod.

slender branch bounces,
relaxing a tired sparrow
newly alighted.

empty cup. across
the room window eye. birds sail
past, my thinking wings.

sweet smoke of morning
dreams. I hear my beating heart,
alarm clock ticking.

Green Park

Today I walked through the warm Green Park
And saw two masters smiling at their hounds.
The one was large, Alsatian; the other, tiny white.
The little one cavorted round his massive friend
And nipped, and barked, and led him merry chase.
The larger one would shrug, then run, then stop,
And wait again for little teasing teeth.
I enjoyed watching the triumph of the smaller dog, as he
    played about the larger one;
But more than this, I enjoyed watching the larger dog allow
    himself to be played with by the smaller.

When I move, the world does not move with me.
Like an orange peel loosely torn from its pulp,
My gaze removes itself from what I see
And looks elsewhere into the supple air.
The buildings stay in place when I walk by,
The brick and concrete firmly joined for centuries;
And passing through a sturdy brace of trees,
I hear and see the gentle, shimmering hiss above,
As a million leafy eyes enjoy the light
In ways that pull aloft their slow woodenness,
Unmindful of myself or other quick-breathing ones
Who play and live around them, or pass in haste beneath.
If I unbutton the cuff of my shirt,
Or stand in a crowd and remember an errand,
The gigantic pulse of human life and flesh still surges;
Someone may jostle me, and continue nimbly on his way.
My world may spread no further than my open arms,
And only one warm kiss may enter it for only one warm
    minute,
And hair and lips and eyelids mingle for only seconds,
But it is eternal, and always new;
And it leaves me forever, and always lasts.
To feel so loose and so dependent;
To know that we must share and be alone;
To feel oneself minute and nestled in a world so huge,
It is as though the past were an ancient trunk,
And our present life were like those trembling leaves
Among which living creatures come and go.

You are reading this, going on and on to the next word;
    or
You are here, with these lines in front of you, reading.

See the difference?

८ Jack

Let us suppose, little Jack, that we have changed our places,
That I have somehow slipped into your little body,
And you have smoothly eased into my own across the aisle,
Where, on this train from Greenwich to Charing Cross those
    five years past,
You sat and gazed across the Thames, a bath of morning light
About you, and the whole compartment rattled in repose,
Until my mother and myself, with her three friends and their
    young daughters,
Clambered on and occupied the seats around you;
And there was much of bustling and shuffling coats and
    laughing,
And pleading for candy when we all had settled in
(My mother placed my by the aisle, across and opposite from
    you);
My right hand held a fat roll of candies, my fingers just
    around it;
The giant seat engulfed me, the armrest next my cheek,
My legs straight out, not even near the edge, the cushioned
    back rising way, way up –
And oh! The lurch and shudder of the iron!
"Going now!" I said, not at all assuming that I was not heard.
And no doubt by this time your eyes were full upon me,
Though never once had I a sense of this.
I grinded at my candies, and went from next to next,
So eager to swallow one flavor and rush upon another;
And soon my body heaved forward and bounced back
    against the seat,
And then I saw that all the bigger people's shoulders jounced
    around
(Yet since they never did acknowledge this, then neither
    would I ever);
"Stopped now," I said and heard the click and chunk of
    doors,
And people came, and cold air, and someone's coat brushed
    against my face,

And then again a shudder, and "Going now" I had to say once
    more;
And as another candy piece would pop into my mouth from
    my sticky hand,
So had I heard my mother say, "We stopped to let more
    people on."
I seldom turned my head, but kept eyes wide and always
    started to laugh.
I was not curious, or would have sometime met your look,
For now your head was turned, and you kept a steady gaze
    upon me;
Your eye was calm and your expression quite impassive;
You shifted your attention now and then, a glance aside,
A skim about your book, a yawn and brief appraisal of the
    sky,
But back you came and looked at me, who watched everyone
And heard them talk about the zoo and soon remembered
    monkeys
And tucked my hand up under my ribs and "Oo loo loo,"
    I cried,
To me a perfect replica of them "Oo loo."
Across the way you were so still,
More quiet than the men immersed in their news items,
More quiet than I would ever want to be.
And so we rode, and the iron clanked and thudded,
And the girls and women talked and ever talked,
And my candies were gone and someone took the wrapper,
And I just sat, my two arms at my side,
My palms flat down upon the sturdy cushion.
And soon the forward heave had slackened low,
And up the big people stood and donned their coats and
    cloaks,
And girls were lifted, and two hands cupped under my
    armpits,
And up I went and saw my mother's face,
Then looped around and down athwart her hip,
Her one arm hooked secure around my waist,

And we went quickly out. The door was shut.
I stared down at more wrappers on the pavement,
And saw a lot of shoes rush by with clicking heels,
And there was iron thunder, and waves and waves of
        shouting,
And so I had not seen you ride away, saw not your face
That, as the train had yawed and pulled along,
Pressed closer to the glass to catch a final glimpse of me.
No, no, I did not see. I soon slipped down into a little stroller
And rolled along out through the leg and shouting forest.
And you had gone somewhere, and since I heard no call,
No mention of my name, I did not turn and look at you,
And so I would not recognize you more.

How curious it is that I would say this.
That I had sat and reconsidered
All the work I have composed;
Reviewed my poems, attempts at feeling,
Attempts at capturing their sweetness.
Reread experiments, descriptions,
Reread, and let them speak to me;
And thought of other words to utter,
And thought of all the silence left,
And felt so bitter at the effort.
Oh yes, so bitter it became.
A drop of acid did it seem,
A hollow clamor in my heart.
I held a sheaf of written sheets.
I held a labor and its wishes.
And words could not prevent the silence,
An empty space around my heart.
It was nothing. It said nothing.
It was all a foolish dream.
We please ourselves with tender phrases
And with the rhymes of cleverness.
I wanted to regret each second,
And to regret each aspiration,
And see just what a fool I was.
All of this paper... am I alive?
Have I ever been sincere?

But how curious it is,
That I would say this now.
That I would sit and write this down,
Addressing it to you who read,
Or you who hear. I speak to you.
I want it said.
I will keep this sheet, and recopy it.
How curious.

*Do not speak
Do not

Whenever you do
Do not

When you would voice what uprears
Do not speak
When you would say what appears
Say not
Do not speak
Do not

When you would undraw the line of her smile,
Untell the cipher in her sigh,
Unplace the whisper in your breast,
No, do not,
No
When the violin string shimmers from ear to entrails as the
        sure bow sings across your heart,
When through a mild haze a curl of smoke lazes and fades
        above the folding green hills,
When a tincture of sunlight flutters tremulous on pressed
        linen,
No, no

When above you massive wet hulks burgeon waywardly
        south like sleeping boulders,
When among the pine tops two crows like hoodlums flap
        shrewdly from branch to wagging branch,
When swallows dive angling in the limpid twilight,
When in midsummer you feel the lilt of evening air, and taste
        abandon in its mature swell,
Oh,

When a nightingale's intimate musings dot the crystal ether
        like quiet phantom stars,
When the last ice patches drip from eaves and branches,
        solitary and reluctant,

When on autumn nights the moody bowers shed their secret
    perfume with a teeming hiss,
When sea foam recedes in burbles and your bare soles press
    the swiftly drying sheen of pliant earth,
When the violet dawn invades the vacant courts and alleys
    with mischief and song;

When you would almost laugh, and the surge tickles you to
    splay merry disorder,
When you would almost weep, and the surge begs your hot
    eyes to explain,
When you would almost mouth your passion, and all of you
    is loud but for the words;
When you would almost, and you do not,
And you do not with your look, with your brow, with your
    stance, your shrug, your smile, sneeze, groan, gasp, press
    of lip, dart of eye, snatch of air, the arch in your shoulder,
    the tilt of your head, the sway of your hip, the lift in your
    step, the stare in your silence;

And when, oh even when, even when you answer, even when
    you describe, or plead, or assail, or upbraid, murmur,
    lecture, whisper, pronounce, unravel, challenge, extol,
    inquire, attest;
Even so, even ever so,

But say what you would say, then say not;
And do not speak,
Do not.

I am a criminal, I should be in chains;
I am the one who hates you when you love yourself,
The one who hates you even when you hate yourself,
The one who watches for the weakness in your eye
Or the tremble of your voice or hand,
The one who knows just when I am unseen
And so remove what I wish, or indulge what I wish;
I am he who has never asked for pity,
Who assures himself that love is opportunity,
And opportunities unfound were no doubt never there.
I am he who listens, who is patient, who troubles no one,
Who only wants his turn, then simply his own corner,
Who keeps you on his corner's threshold and nods at you
from there.
I am he who kills; I have murdered many,
I have beaten many others and humiliated many more,
The clench in my jaw reveals it, or my silence in society,
Or my busy days, or my open book, or my food.
(Have you never realized who lingers there, hooded and
unseen?
Would you but ever pull back the cowl and scream an
accusation to the crowd!)
I am not hunted, I am not played with,
I am not asked to dinner, I am not kissed,
I am never, never begged to
(Good thing, for I would only laugh);
I am not pursued, I am too sly for that,
I wear a suit of clothes like you, and I speak like you,
I walk among you all, among you ants and monkeys;
You only see yourself when you look at me,
This, the final protection: to be always a mirror,
To be always you, always what you want and what you do not
want;
How strangely clever is the world, to make us each a god of
our own liking,
To make us each believe that every gesture from the crowd
Is meant to please us, or to hail us, or to show us something
new.
But I do not feel this way, I know what fools you are.

I am not pursued, no, how could you chase what never needs
    to run?
If they caught me – they will never catch me – but if they did,
They would chain me like a lion, with irons round my neck
    and limbs;
They would be cautious, for I would bite and kick;
And they would use long poles with sharpened blades
To force me in a corner and shut the door before it,
And I would spit and thrash, and throw myself against the
    door,
And the door would shudder, and the bolts and hinges
    buckle,
And the iron would cut my legs and wrists and neck, and all
    outside would tremble,
And back and forth they'd walk, and look alarmed, and peep
    in through the grate,
And they would see me silent, and would never understand
    how I feel.

⟲ My Diary

I cannot keep a diary.
If I were to say what had happened today,
And told you of my bath, and breakfast, and other bodily
    habits;
Or mentioned my day's mail, and my musings thereon;
Or recounted my phone calls, and my feelings for those to
    whom I spoke,
And the mystery of who they are, and what we mean to each
    other;
If you read of my shopping, and of my post office visit,
And were there with me as I jaunted along the teeming street,
The world alive with neglect of who I am;
Had you grumbled with me as I sought out an empty chair in
    the café,
Or sidled through the aisles as we selected a new shirt for
    summer,
Or pored over my verse, and here struck out a word and
    there another inserted;
Were you to marvel with me at the strange resemblance of
    these events to many of your own,
Were you to wonder why I would write of mine, when I could
    as well seek you out, and talk to you,
And write in detail of your post office visits, and showers and
    coffee,
And your friends, and mail unanswered, and someone you
    love dearly,
And whether cotton or wool best suited your wardrobe,
And if you would lunch, or wait until evening, or nap or not,
I think you'd agree, had you perused a page, or more than a
    page, of them,
I think you'd agree that there was indeed no point at all
In my preserving in the blank leaves of a stitched up volume
A sequence of days and nights, of habit remembered and
    dialogue captured,
Of impulses followed, and others pursued but in thought,
Of long, long passages of silence, of my breathing, alone,

Of sunlight, sounds of traffic, distracted look of someone
    speaking,
Of evening joys and fears, the sweet smothered breast and
    lingering flame;
Yes, to place this in ordered paragraphs and entitle the
    summation of it all "My Diary,"
Were as if to sketch myself without a glass, and the lines and
    shading mount in guesses,
And there is more of what is drawn than what is seen.

To All the Thoughts

To all the thoughts that slipped away,
Amid a chat, or gazing out a window, or alone with a book,
Or lying quiet in the night,
Suddenly a whisper, a heart-lifting word, a moment bright
    with new fire,
A definite idea, or story, or image to work out in detail,
An elusive yet solid flutter of insight,
And somehow, it was not noted down;
No paper to hand, or pen, or time (or illusion of no time),
Or, regrettable to say, no push against ennui;
It was so solid, it filled brightly this one minute,
I will articulate it, later.
I will remember it, later.
It will come back.
And it was gone.
What was solid, and near to me, and glowing with unknown
    colors,
Gone.
It will not come back.

To all the thoughts that were embraced,
The pinprick of understanding, the heartfelt shimmer rising,
Oh, stop what you are doing,
Find a scrap, a cardboard box top, the wall,
Write it down now, write enough so you remember how it
    felt,
So you can later spread out and arrange its dancing points,
So later you can carve the line, or pages, or song, to arouse
    again and ever again that shimmer, that rising;
And there they lay for months, for years,
The ragged cardboard with its hasty lines,
The scribble in a corner of the page,
The scribble all about the page,
The folded pieces, in red and black and blue ink,
A thought embraced (one hopes the moment too was
    embraced),

A thought that, in its rushed arrival, rests and rests, and will
  so rest, sung only once on the incidental scrap that
  holds it.

To all the thoughts that were a seed,
A phantom nothing so it seemed,
An idle word from someone, or a change of light upon the
  grass,
A looming picture in the mind (where did you come from?),
A yearning, then a plan, then a duty, to make solid what
  appeared.
And it too was written down,
Or it was not written down,
But still, it breathed when you did,
And it walked where you walked,
And it said what you said,
Until the time arrived when you said what it said,
When it stopped you, and set you down, and ruled your life,
  and starved and thirsted you,
Until its chords were struck, its housel shaped and offered,
  its stops and strings honed true,
And it sang and became what it was,
And it taught you who it was, and who you are.

To all the thoughts that were also a seed,
A knife-like moment of clear undoubt,
A lucid epic tale the heart unravels in one instant,
A poem so complete that, to give it voice,
To even look about for pen and ink,
Would be its end;
And it rules you, and it loves you,
And you will love, this once, at least this once,
And where you are, and what you see, and who you are with,
Become the ink, the line, the page,
This poem in the leaf of this one moment sits,
This poem that, only unspoke, unwrit, untold, may sing.

To all the thoughts that are a servant:
To all the thoughts that were a chalice,
Holding the beaming wine of knowledge,
The sure moment understood and breathing,
Again we sip, and know, and feel without speaking,
And without the need to speak;
To all the thoughts that were a taper,
Strike and spark, then flame both soft and fiendish,
Ruthless in its need to burn, to brighten and make living,
And they quiver, and know, and feel without speaking,
And without the need to speak;
To all the thoughts that are a chalice, now, and are a taper,
    now,
They are writ on scraps of silence,
They know no ennui or panic,
They are embraced, and lay tucked away, and yet are ever
    opened and read, and newly teach, and fold away again,
They are trimmed and honed and sculpted,
And they sing themselves,
And they blaze themselves,
And they breathe and they walk and they regard,
And they have no need of ink, or notepads,
And they arrive, elude, depart,
Chalice and flame, what holds and offers, what ignites and
    forges;
To all these thoughts that, once alive, may sough away at
    once,
Never to be uttered, never could be uttered,
Their precious epistle this incitement to appear,
To make solid this touch, this breath, this beat of the hour,
Then we, no longer phantom, no longer eluded, no longer
    tucked away,
We arrive, we this thought arrive, embraced and writ, and
    living.

www.ingramcontent.com/pod-product-compliance
Lightning Source LLC
Chambersburg PA
CBHW062033040426

42447CB00010B/2266